This page intentionally left blank

Purple Flowers in Bloom: A Coloring and Activity Guide for Using Emotions to Be Colorfully Creative

This guide offers a unique opportunity to identify and express emotions in a creative and colorful way. By using your preferred coloring tools, such as watercolors, coloring pencils, crayons, paints, canvas, and brushes, you can truly immerse yourself in the activities provided.

To enhance your experience, we recommend considering the use of music, candles, or other positive stimuli to set the mood. The guide is designed to encourage the expression of emotions in a comfortable, enjoyable, and authentic manner.

We hope that this guide will provide you with a sense of creative fulfillment and encourage you to explore your emotions in a new and exciting way.

© 2023 Akeelah Publishing House
Trisheena Bolakale
Purple Flowers In Bloom: A Coloring and Activity Guide for Using Emotions to Be Colorfully Creative
All rights reserved. No part of this publication may be reproduced, stored in a retrieval system or transmitted in any form or by any means, electronic, mechanical, photocopying, recording or otherwise without the prior permission of the publisher or in accordance with the provisions of the Copyright, Designs and Patents Act 1988 or under the terms of any licence permitting limited copying issued by the Copyright Licensing Agency.
Published by: Akeelah Publishing House
Text Design by: Trisheena Bolakale
Cover Design by: Trisheena Bolakale
A CIP record for this book is available from the Library of Congress Cataloging-in-Publication Data
ISBN-13: 979-8-9876772-1-6

Warmth

AGGRESSION

RED

LOVE

RAGE

passion

Let your creativity flow, it's time to create!

Paint a mountain peak with a tree in the valley. Your mountaintop will represent you at your highest point and the tree in the valley will represent the struggles you are facing. Express your thoughts through your painting or drawing.

There is a blank page for your creation

COLD

tranquility

freedom

BLUE

SADNESS

STABILITY

depression

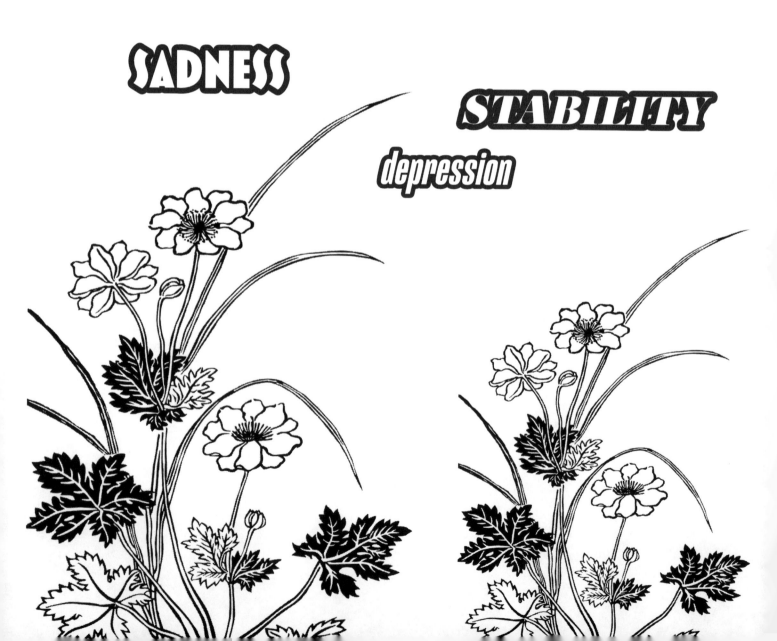

Let your creativity flow, it's time to create!

Send a Balloon to Heaven...
Do you have someone in heaven that you want to send a message to? Draw a picture of a balloon and color a message inside of it.

There is a blank page for your creation

HEALTH

HAPPINESS

desolation

ENTHUSIASM

Ruin

ORANGE

fun

DANGER

creativity

cheerfulness

energetic

optemism

joy

YELLOW

warmth

FRIENDLINESS

Let your creativity flow, it's time to create!

Draw a Heart.
How about expressing your love in a more creative way? Draw a heart and infuse it with the color of your love. Let your heart speak the language of love!

There is a blank page for your creation

POISON LUCK
NATURE growth
CORRUPTION
hope Green

envy PROSPERITY

ROMANCE

INNOCENCE

immaturity

kind

deception

delicate

MATERIALISM

SWEET

PINK

Let your creativity flow, it's time to create!

Make a Collage of Happy Colors

Create a work of art using all of the colors that you identify as happy colors. Get creative! A bouquet of Pink and Purple Flowers sounds so devine.

There is a blank page for your creation

ROMANCE   FUTURE

mystery

ROYALTY   detachment

attraction

spirituality   luxury

PURPLE

Let your creativity flow, it's time to create!

Self Portrait- How Do YOU See Yourself?

Paint a picture representing how you see yourself. Think of the colors that you want to use. Consider the structure that you want to use. Do you see yourself as a vessel? Be sure to connect with yourself as you complete this activity.

There is a blank page for your creation

This page intentionally left blank

Let your creativity flow, it's time to create!

Finger Paint

Remember this activity? Heal your inner child and get dirty using finger paints. Use the colors and your emotions to guide this painting.

There is a blank page for your creation

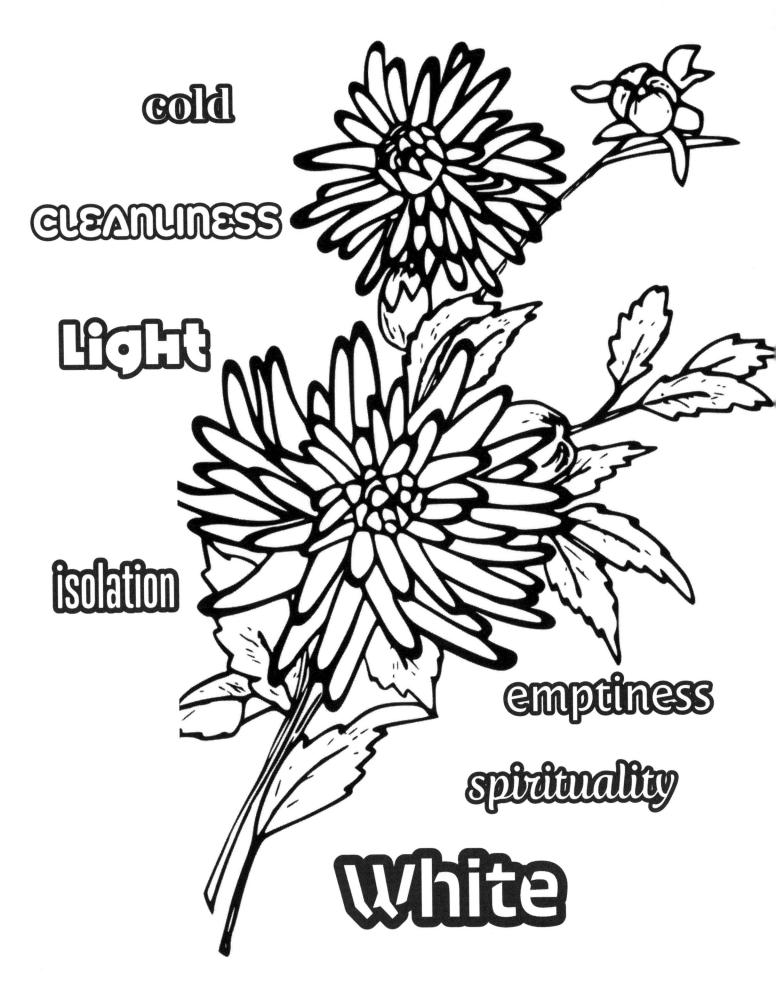

AUTHORITY

TIMELINESS

calm

neutrality

DULL

STABILITY

STRENGTH

Grey

What am I supposed to do with this rage? they say don't have rage! But I do!! So, what now? this RAGE is red hot, but orange has it a lot more mellow. Moving slowly rage starts to turn a deepish color yellow. And this rage is turning green, let it be your safety, don't ignore this rage, let love drive it where it needs to be. Blue is setting in trust yourself to work it through. it's ok to own the rage

Don't let the rage own you.

Now with this rage, I'm in a garden and surrounded by the flowers.
but the purple ones have given rage's love a different power.
So, this rage though forbidden by those who came before me sits proudly in my garden blooming love so
FREELY.

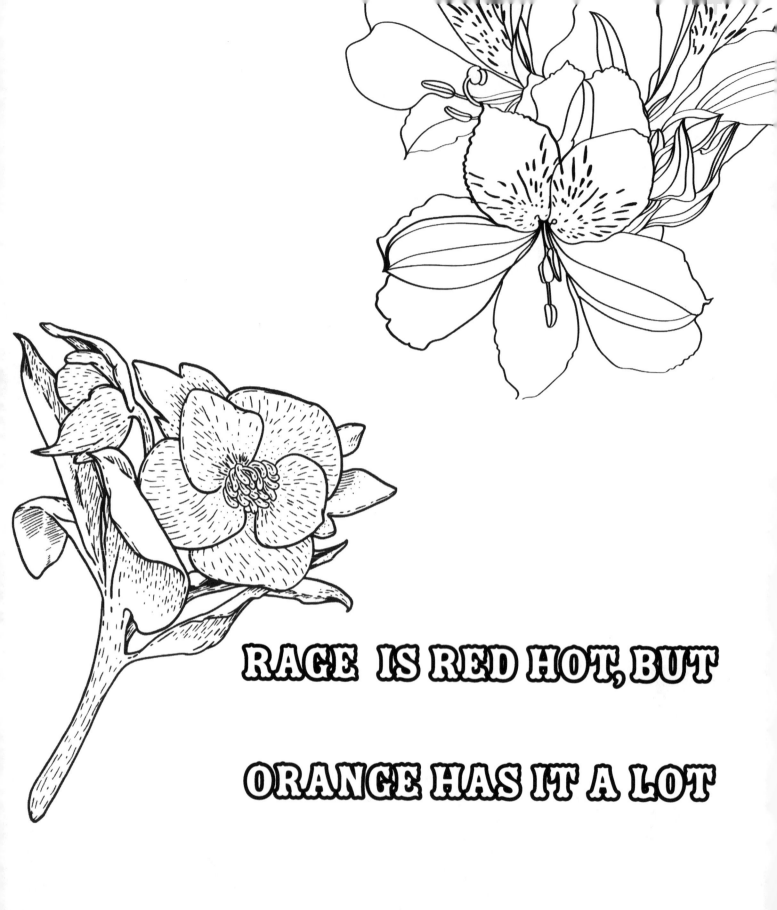

RAGE IS RED HOT, BUT

ORANGE HAS IT A LOT

MORE MELLOW,

MOVING SLOWLY RAGE STARTS TO A DEEPISH COLOR YELLOW.

AND THIS RAGE IS TURNING GREEN, LET THAT BE YOUR SAFETY

DON'T IGNORE THIS RAGE, LET LOVE DRIVE IT WHERE IT NEEDS TO BE.

BLUE IS SETTING IN TRUST YOURSELF TO WORK IT THROUGH.

IT'S OK TO OWN THE RAGE.
DON'T LET THE RAGE OWN YOU.

NOW WITH THIS RAGE
I'M IN A GARDEN AND
SURROUNDED BY THE FLOWERS,
BUT THE PURPLE ONES HAVE GIVEN
RAGE'S LOVE A DIFFERENT POWER.

GREY
Blue
Purple
Yellow
Relaxation
White
Pink

Let your creativity flow, it's time to create!

Draw or Paint a New invention!
Think of something that would make your lif eeasier, it can be a structure or use colors that would be most helpful to you. Turn this "invention" into art!

There is a blank page for your creation

Let your creativity flow, it's time to create!

Have You Ever Had a Spiritual Experience?
Paint a picture representing how you felt and what it meant to you.

There is a blank page for your creation

Let your creativity flow, it's time to create!

Draw or paint a comic strip book about your prom night or another important night.

What colors can be used to paint this memory? How do you see yourself in this memory? Turn this important time into art!

There is a blank page for your creation

Let your creativity flow, it's time to create!

Collage of Love Lost

Think about a person or another love that you may have lost. Paint your feelings as you process those emotions.

There is a blank page for your creation

Colors that express...

BLUE

YELLOW

GREEN

SELF-IMAGE

Colors that express...

Let your creativity flow, it's time to create!

Draw something that Scares you.
What brings you fear? Think about the colors that you want to use.

There is a blank page for your creation

Let your creativity flow, it's time to create!

Draw or Paint an Important Childhood Memory

Think about an important day in your childhood. Bring colors to that memory and turn it into art.

There is a blank page for your creation

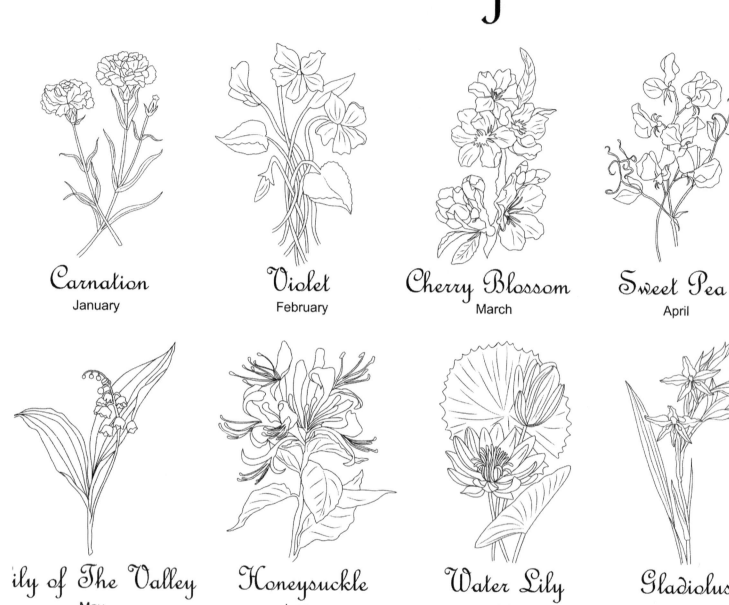

GROUNDING ACTIVITY

Take a moment to breathe deeply and meditate for two minutes to center yourself. You can light a candle or incense to set the mood. Take a terra cotta flower pot and fill it halfway with soil. Leave all your insecurities and anything that brings you pain in the dirt. As you work the soil with your hands, let it become your strength. Take a seed and plant it in the soil. This seed represents your growth and potential. Speak words of love and peace into your growth as you cover the seed with two inches of soil. Water your pot and repeat those affirmations over your plant. Cover the pot with Saran Wrap and place it on a sunny windowsill where it can receive plenty of sunlight.

Let your creativity flow, it's time to create!

Turn your Illness into Art
Are you struggling with a visible or invisible illness? Express your emotions through art and turn your illness into color!

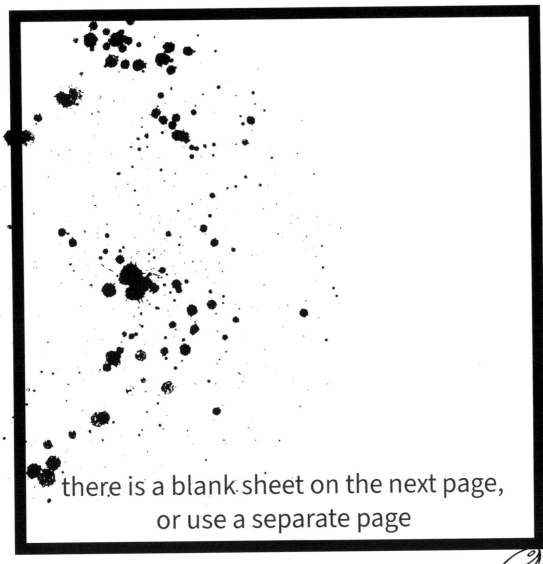

there is a blank sheet on the next page, or use a separate page

Pink

GRATITUDE

RAGE

What am I supposed to do with this rage?
They say don't have rage! But I do!! So
what now?
this rage is red hot, but orange has it a lot
more mellow. Moving slowly rage starts to
turn a deepish color yellow.
And this rage is turning green, let it be
your safety. Don't ignore this rage, let love
drive it where it needs to be.
Blue is setting in trust yourself to work it
through. It's okay to own the rage
Don't let the rage own you.
Now with this rage, I'm in a garden and
surrounded by the flowers.,
but the purple ones have given rages love
a different power.
So, this rage though forbidden by those
who came before me sits proudly in my
garden blooming
love so freely.

By Trisheena Bolakale

Made in the USA
Middletown, DE
21 June 2024

55769311R00046